"Overcome evil with good,
falsehood with truth,
and hatred with love."
—Peace Pilgrim

Walking toward
PEACE

The True Story of a Brave Woman
Called Peace Pilgrim

KATHLEEN KRULL

Illustrated by
ANNIE BOWLER

flyaway
books

The world was weary with war. Meanwhile, a mysterious woman decided to walk.

She had a good life. She enjoyed expensive dresses and fancy shoes. She liked her friends. But one evening, while taking a moonlit walk in the woods, she had a sudden and surprising thought. She didn't care about money anymore. What she really wanted was a life that mattered. She wanted to find a way to make the world better.

Her greatest fear was that the country would fall into wartime chaos. But what could one person do about that? Into her mind came a map of the United States. She imagined a crayon as it drew a line from coast to coast. It gave her the idea to walk—as a pilgrim for peace.

She decided to give up her real name and everything she owned. Peace Pilgrim would be her new name, and her goal was to walk twenty-five thousand miles.

Step by step, she would make this pilgrimage happen. And somehow, in a country that could think only of war, she would spread peace.

She took years to get ready. To master the skills she would need to survive, she spent many hours in the forest, practicing how to find food and find her way.

Peace started within. As she prepared, she focused on good thoughts and good actions every day. She read to the elderly and helped tend their gardens.

She worked with kids in trouble.

She volunteered with groups that promoted peace.

Finally, she was ready to walk. She celebrated New Year's Day by beginning her pilgrimage. Wearing simple sneakers and a blue shirt printed with her new name, she stepped out in front of the Rose Parade in Pasadena, California. As she walked, she talked to people along the parade route and handed out small printed messages, asking everyone to consider peace.

That was just the beginning.

After the Rose Parade ended, Peace Pilgrim kept walking, one foot in front of the other. The pockets of her shirt held her only possessions: a toothbrush, a comb, a pen, copies of her message, and maps. She never carried money.

Days passed, step by step. She walked joyfully, with purpose and a ready smile. She would stop and talk anywhere, anytime, with anyone interested in her quest. She would explain her goal: a golden age of peace, a world with no fighting between people or nations.

Some people worried. Did she know what she was doing? Was she an outlaw? But many who met her and talked with her were inspired. She spoke in a commonsense way, waking them up. So many people assumed war was a necessary part of life. Peace Pilgrim helped them see that another way might be possible.

She preferred to walk on mountain trails, beaches, paths in the forest—
quiet places where she could talk to a few people at a time.

She cherished the beauty of nature, where every flower and tree seemed to glow.

But when necessary, she walked alongside busy highways to get from place to place.

As she walked through San Diego, she was invited to talk about peace at a school. This began her new life as a public speaker, sharing her message with many more people. But even then, as her audiences grew, she would move on and keep walking. There were always more people to meet, more people to talk to. More and more people wanted to listen.

For a week in Colorado Springs, she talked to a dozen groups, from five people to five hundred people. On one day in Cincinnati, she gave seven sermons at seven different places of worship. She began to write back and forth with strangers whom she made into friends—hundreds of them.

For food, she often relied on kindness. Sometimes she dined at the fanciest hotel in town. Sometimes she enjoyed tortillas and beans at a migrant worker's home. Sometimes nature fed her with apples fallen from trees or wild berries dripping with dew.

She gratefully accepted any offer of shelter. She would sleep on a front porch or the couch of a new friend.

In Arizona, she spent one night on the city hall conference table and another on the front seat of a fire engine.

Other times, she slept at bus stops or truck stops or on the grass beside the road. One of her favorite places was a haystack, under a blanket of stars.

Step by step, Peace Pilgrim crossed from the West Coast to the East Coast, talking to people about peace everywhere she went. Nearly a year after her start in Pasadena, she made it to New York City. There she saw the United Nations Building, home to the new world peace-keeping organization, and she spent her nights sleeping at the Grand Central train station.

This was her first pilgrimage. But she wasn't finished.

It would take much longer to reach her goal of twenty-five thousand miles. So, after rest and more preparation, she began anew.

For her second pilgrimage, Peace Pilgrim started from San Francisco. She tried to walk at least a hundred miles and visit the capital in each state she visited, and she also crossed into Mexico and Canada.

Finally, in Washington, DC, she succeeded. She had walked twenty-five thousand miles, all to ask people to consider peace.

After that, she stopped counting the miles, but she never stopped walking.

Step by step, east and west, north and south, she zigzagged across the country. Like a bird, she traveled south in the fall and north in the spring. During walk after walk, she never got sick, seemed to have no fear, and was rarely in danger. Strangers continued to help. In freezing Oklahoma, a student gave her his gloves and scarf.

On the coldest nights, she walked all night in order to keep warm. On the hottest days, she walked at night to stay cool, surrounded by fireflies, loving the smell of nature blossoming around her. She kept on walking through dust storms, rainfall, and snowstorms.

Peace Pilgrim made it to all fifty states. Supporters helped her get to Alaska, leading a tour that inspired many to return home and start working to help others. In Hawaii, she slept on the beach, cooked over campfires, and gathered people together to sing.

On holidays, she would take a break and catch up on her mail. "Greetings from South Dakota!" she would write, or "Iowa" or "Minnesota."

She spent one Christmas in New Orleans and another in Fort Worth, Texas.

Years passed, step by step. Averaging twenty-five miles a day, she wore out twenty-nine pairs of sneakers.

How many miles can a person walk for peace? Though she stopped counting, Peace Pilgrim kept walking for *twenty-eight years*. How many pilgrimages can one person make? She crisscrossed the country *seven times*.

Peace Pilgrim thought of walking as a prayer—a prayer for peace. Everywhere she went, she invited people to act in ways that would make the world a more peaceful place. And, step by step, they did.

PEACE PILGRIM

Peace Pilgrim was born Mildred Lisette Norman in 1908 in Egg Harbor City, New Jersey. She grew up on a chicken farm, surrounded by a forest she could play in and a creek she could swim in.

After graduating at the top of her high school class and as head of the debate team, she worked as a secretary. With an active social life, she dressed at the height of fashion and always had her shoes dyed to match her dress and gloves.

She came to consider this an empty life and began preparing for her new goal. In 1953, at the age of forty-four, she began her first pilgrimage walk, starting her path toward becoming a peace activist and spiritual teacher.

Occasionally she was arrested for vagrancy, a crime defined as wandering around without a home or a job. She would be released when she explained to police what she was doing or when friends vouched for her. A friend back in Egg Harbor City forwarded her mail whenever she was in one place long enough to receive it; this helped her keep in touch with all her new friends.

Peace Pilgrim had lived through the nightmarish global conflict of World War II, and over her years of walking, she opposed the Korean War, the Cold War, the Vietnam War, and the nuclear arms race. She considered war the greatest evil of her time. A frequent speaker in churches and schools, she also enjoyed being interviewed on radio and TV—anywhere she could talk about peace.

Throughout the middle years of the twentieth century, her voice was part of a growing chorus singing in resistance to war. "Violence never brings permanent peace," declared civil rights leader Martin Luther King Jr. "Nonviolence takes more guts, if I can put it bluntly, than violence," said Cesar Chavez, labor leader and civil rights activist. President John F. Kennedy said, "Mankind must put an end to war, or war will put an end to mankind." Another president, Lyndon B. Johnson, said, "The guns and the bombs, the rockets and the warships, are all symbols of human failure."

Never interested in retiring, Peace Pilgrim had speaking engagements booked all the way to early 1984. She sometimes accepted rides to get to a speech, and in 1981, during her seventh pilgrimage, she died in a car accident in Indiana. She was seventy-two.

But her work lived on. In 2019, she was among twelve women honored by the National Women's History Alliance as "Visionary Women: Champions of Peace and Nonviolence." Although the world still struggles with war, Peace Pilgrim's message of peace has echoed through time.

SOURCES

Peace Pilgrim. *Peace Pilgrim: Her Life and Work in Her Own Words*. Santa Fe, NM: Ocean Tree Books, 2004.

National Women's History Alliance, "2019 Honorees," https://nationalwomenshistoryalliance.org/2019-honorees/.

Peace Pilgrim official website, https://www.peacepilgrim.org.

For my niece Allison Krull, already on the path
—K. K.

For Peter, always
—A. B.

Text © 2021 Kathleen Krull
Illustrations © 2021 Anne Bowler

First edition
Published by Flyaway Books
Louisville, Kentucky

21 22 23 24 25 26 27 28 29 30–10 9 8 7 6 5 4 3 2 1

Book design by Allison Taylor
Text set in PMN Caecilia

Library of Congress Cataloging-in-Publication Data
Names: Krull, Kathleen, author. | Bowler, Annie, illustrator.
Title: Walking toward peace : the true story of a brave woman called peace
    pilgrim / Kathleen Krull ; illustrated by Annie Bowler.
Description: First Edition. | Louisville : Flyaway Books, 2021. | Audience:
    Ages 3-7 | Audience: Grades K-1 | Summary: "Tells the true story of
    Peace Pilgrim, a female activist and spiritual leader who sacrificed
    everything to travel by foot around America promoting peace"-- Provided
    by publisher.
Identifiers: LCCN 2020029070 (print) | LCCN 2020029071 (ebook) | ISBN
    9781947888265 (hardback) | ISBN 9781646980369 (ebook)
Subjects: LCSH: Peace Pilgrim, -1981. | Women pacifists--United
    States--Juvenile literature.
Classification: LCC JZ5538 .K78 2021 (print) | LCC JZ5538 (ebook) | DDC
    303.6/6 [B]--dc23
LC record available at https://lccn.loc.gov/2020029070
LC ebook record available at https://lccn.loc.gov/2020029071

PRINTED IN CHINA

Most Flyaway Books are available at special quantity discounts when purchased in bulk by corporations, organizations, and special-interest groups. For more information, please e-mail SpecialSales@flyawaybooks.com.